Original title:
Blush of the Blossom

Copyright © 2025 Creative Arts Management OÜ
All rights reserved.

Author: Atticus Thornton
ISBN HARDBACK: 978-1-80567-010-0
ISBN PAPERBACK: 978-1-80567-090-2

The Carnation's Secret Smile

In the garden, secrets hide,
A carnation grins, feeling spry.
With petals like a cheeky wink,
It giggles softly, just a blink.

Amongst the daisies, it's a tease,
Whispering jokes on a summer breeze.
No one knows its playful ruse,
Just a floral with clever views.

Fuchsia Sunbeams at Noon

Fuchsia blooms dance in the heat,
Swinging their petals to a funky beat.
They swap their colors for some fun,
And throw a party under the sun.

Each petal tells a silly tale,
Of funky hats and ships that sail.
Underneath the noon's bright gaze,
Petals bounce in playful ways.

The Subtle Art of Blooming

To bloom or not, that's the quest,
A flower's life is quite a jest.
With colors bright and fragrance bold,
They strut their stuff, a sight to behold.

They wink at bees, who buzz and flit,
A dance of pollen, oh, what a hit!
While leaves turn green with envy, too,
The art of blooming steals the view.

Illusions of Petal Grace

Petals twirl like ballerinas,
Wearing skirts of bright hyacinths.
With every gust, they take a chance,
To show off moves in a floral dance.

But oh, the wind can be so sly,
It lifts them up and makes them fly!
They tumble down with giggles loud,
An audience of bugs so proud.

The Language of Colorful Whispers

In a garden where giggles grow,
Petals gossip, putting on a show.
Each hue has a tale, so vivid and bright,
Chasing clouds with laughter, what a sight!

Dandelions dance, oh what a fuss,
While daisies tease with a cheeky bus.
Their colors squabble, who's best dressed?
In this palette of fun, we're all blessed!

Swaying with the Spring Breeze

Grass tickles toes in a playful fling,
Trees sway along, they know how to sing.
Breezes giggle, rustling all around,
While flowers throw confetti on the ground.

With petals like hats, they join in the spree,
Do you think tulips are sipping sweet tea?
In their cheerful chatter, joy intertwines,
Nature's oddball party, oh how it shines!

Blooming Dreams in Soft Light

Morning dew drips like a cheeky tease,
As sunbeams tickle the sleeping trees.
Each bud whispers secrets in morning grace,
While shadows play hide and seek in space.

Butterflies waltz, oh what a delight,
They glide through the air, a whimsical flight.
With laughter in petals, they float and dream,
In this world of whimsy, it's all a gleam!

Painted Faces of Nature

Nature's makeup is quite a mess,
With splashes of color, it's anyone's guess.
Roses pout, and the violets wink,
While sunflowers strut, quicker than you think.

Cherries blush with a cheeky grin,
As bees buzz around, ready to win.
Each fruit and flower has a quip to share,
Painting the world like an artist with flair!

Crimson Kisses on Morning Dew

In the garden, a ticklish breeze,
Flowers giggle and sway with ease.
Bees buzz by, wearing their hats,
Chasing ants who dance with spats.

A frog in the pond gives a loud croak,
While daisies whisper the latest joke.
Sunlight drips like syrupy honey,
While bumblebees laugh, 'Ain't this funny?'

Enchanted Petals at Twilight

Under the moon, the petals twirl,
A butterfly spins and gives a whirl.
Crickets join in, a charming band,
Even the shadows begin to dance grand.

Somehow, a cat gets caught in twine,
While roses plot a silly line.
'Who left the snacks?' they start to plot,
'Let's eat till we can't move a spot!'

Fragrant Echoes of New Beginnings

A daffodil sneezed and startled a bee,
Who buzzed away saying, 'Not on me!'
Tulips gossip about spider webs,
While laughing at clouds in fluffy ebbs.

The sun peeks out, a playful chap,
Joking with shadows, taking a nap.
'Next time,' he says, 'ask me to play!'
But it's curtains for clouds, come what may.

Rosy Hues at Daybreak

As dawn breaks, the pinks rise high,
A tomato plant claims it can fly.
Petunias roll their eyes with flair,
Declaring, 'Oh please, we're beyond compare!'

A squirrel laughs, doing a jig,
While the sun rolls out in a bright, warm gig.
Roots stretch long, sharing tales of fun,
While morning laughs, 'Don't forget to run!'

Petals' Soft Embrace

In gardens where giggles sway,
The petals dance in a cheeky way.
They play hide and seek with the bees,
Tickling the petals in warm spring breeze.

The tulips wear sassy little hats,
While daisies laugh with their furry cats.
A rose tries to strut with a flair,
But its thorns are just giving me a scare!

Whispering Hues of Spring

Oh look, a daffodil's trying to grin,
With bright yellow cheeks, can it even begin?
The violets joke with a wink and a nod,
While the pansies await their quick brush of God.

It's a color party, a floral delight,
With tulips that giggle at each silly sight.
As bumblebees buzz, trying hard to keep cool,
The blossoms all dance like their own funny school.

The Tender Bloom Awakens

With a yawn that stretches bright,
A blossom wakes up, full of light.
It stumbles out, not quite awake,
And fumbles over a sleepy lake.

Petals toss like a morning bedhair,
They trip and tangle, but show no care.
A pollen sneeze brings a chorus of cheer,
As the flowers all crack up, 'Oh dear, oh dear!'

Scarlet Kiss of Dawn

As dawn paints the skies in crimson cheer,
A cheeky bloom whispers, "Hey, come here!"
It winks to the sun, a playful tease,
"My fragrance is sweeter than all your breeze!"

The tulip trips over its own bright feet,
While daisies do cartwheels—oh, what a treat!
With morning's embrace, they laugh out loud,
In a circus of colors, they're oh so proud!

Veils of Pink in the Garden

In a garden where giggles grow,
Petals sway in a playful show.
Bees in tuxedos buzz with glee,
Dancing round blooms like they're on a spree.

Sunlight kisses the floral crew,
While rabbits plot a prank or two.
A flower sneezes, pollen flies,
The garden erupts in silly sighs.

With petals winking in a breeze,
And squirrels chatting with fluffy ease.
A dandelion's hat goes astray,
As butterflies chuckle at the display.

In this realm of colors so bright,
Nature's jesters come to light.
For every petal that tickles the air,
A smile is born, beyond compare.

A Symphony in Fuchsia

In a world where fuchsia reigns,
A trombone flower plays with gains.
Bouncing blooms, they leap and twist,
While daisies hum a cheeky list.

A rose in pink sings off-key,
While violets giggle with all their glee.
Their laughter floats on breezy tunes,
As frogs join in with silly croons.

Petunias prance, a waltz so grand,
With nature's humor, they take a stand.
Even sunflowers nod and sway,
In this symphony of pure play.

Oh, what a concert, come along!
With blooms so vibrant, it can't be wrong.
For when the petals unite in fun,
The whole garden knows they've won!

Morning's Floral Serenade

Morning breaks with a jovial giggle,
As daisies dance and tulips wiggle.
A sunflower's hat is too big, you see,
While morning glories stretch with glee.

The dew drop drops, a slippery prank,
As pigeons strut in rank and flank.
Bumblebees buzz with a funny tune,
While petals sway, a flowered croon.

A lilac whispers a quirky joke,
As sunlight warms the playful cloak.
The air is filled with floral cheer,
Each leaf chuckles as friends come near.

So here's to mornings bright and bold,
With tales of petals yet untold.
In every hue, a smile's spun,
A floral serenade, all in fun!

The Purity of Petal Palettes

In gardens lush with colors grand,
Petals gather, a merry band.
Roses prank with a sharp thorn tease,
While daisies whisper between the leaves.

White lilies dress up, a comedy show,
As they chuckle at the wind's soft blow.
A tulip trips, falls on its face,
While marigolds giggle, just in case.

With every hue in perfect place,
Nature's canvas wears a cheeky face.
A coral bloom starts a wild trend,
Drawing laughs from every floral friend.

So let the palettes brightness proclaim,
That flowers too can play the game.
In this pure realm of petals' delight,
Life's a laugh, a colorful sight!

The Pink Veil of Dawn

The sun peeks shyly through the trees,
Ducking behind clouds, like a tease.
Birds chirp gossip, oh what a sight,
As flowers giggle at the morning light.

Squirrels in a dance, a humorous show,
Chasing shadows, putting on a glow.
The grass stretches wide, what a stretch!
Each blade a comedian, ready to fetch!

The dew drops sparkle, laughter in air,
Whispering secrets without a care.
Nature's own jesters, funny and frilly,
Their colors so bold, it's almost silly!

Bees buzz around with a humorous glee,
Confused by flowers, oh where's my tea?
The morning's a canvas, absurd and bright,
With a riot of colors that tickle the sight.

Awakening Stains of Spring

A patchwork quilt of colors is spread,
Nature's palette in chaos, widespread.
Dandelions laugh, like clowns in a play,
While tulips tease squirrels to come out and play!

Chirpy little robins, so proud and so bold,
Fashioned in bright hues, a sight to behold.
They strut through the garden, a comical dance,
As blossoms invite them to join in romance.

The wind plays tricks, a practical joke,
Tickling the petals, can't help but provoke.
With each gust, they sway, a humorous waltz,
As if they were jesters, spinning in faults.

Pollen confetti flies with a flair,
Chaque flower's a party, who brought the wear?
Laughing together as spring's song unfolds,
In stains of joy, nature's laughter molds.

Timid Hues of Morning Light

The horizon blushes with colors so strange,
Whispers of orange and shades that rearrange.
A shy daffodil peeks from its bed,
Wondering if the world is still asleep, or dead.

Butterflies flutter, all dressed in their best,
Winging around flowers, a whimsical quest.
The daisies giggle as they make their stand,
While tulips gossip about a flower band.

The sun turns up loud, a boisterous blast,
Awakening all, a party to last.
Hues dance about, in a bright, silly spree,
Like jesters on stage, singing carefree!

A breeze brings a chuckle, rustling the leaves,
As nature chuckles and the world believes.
Morning's a jester, a spectacle bright,
With timidly proud hues claiming the light.

The Poetry Hidden in Petals

In petals of pink, a mystery lies,
Stories of laughter, whispers, and sighs.
Bees compose verses, penned in their buzz,
While flowers recite, 'Hey, just because!'

The marigolds mock the roses in bloom,
While tulips provide a colorful room.
Nature's own scribes, short rhymes in a row,
Each petal a line, a poetic show!

Poppies waltz softly, ticked by the breeze,
With daffodils laughing, as lightens the tease.
Their colors collide, forming a tight wrap,
Where jokes are well-kept, all crammed into sap.

So ponder the petals, what tales do they tell?
Of laughter in gardens where colors dwell.
In each vibrant whisper, from root to the tip,
A funny little sonnet takes a lively trip!

Fading Echoes of Floral Beauty

In the garden, flowers giggle,
Petals dance, a funny wiggle.
Bees buzz loud, in a silly race,
Smelling sweet like a cupcake's face.

Leaves whisper secrets, oh so light,
The sun peeks in, a cheeky sight.
They plot and scheme, these blooms so bold,
Colorful tales of laughter told.

Melody of Petals in the Wind

Petals flit like feathered jesters,
In their playful, breezy festers.
They swirl and twirl, just like a dream,
Catching giggles in a sunbeam.

Dandelions puff with cheeky glee,
Waving goodbye, 'come hug me, see?'
As sunlight drips with a honeyed tease,
The flowers chuckle in the soft breeze.

A Palette of Nature's Embrace

Colors clash in a vibrant brawl,
Red and yellow trying to enthrall.
A daisy pokes a tulip's head,
'You think you're fancy? Let's be fed!'

The petals wear hats, some quite absurd,
'Look at me now!' a rosebird stirred.
Laughing blooms, in a joyous race,
A vibrant hug of nature's grace.

Moments Caught in Blooming Glow

In the glade, where flowers boast,
A poppy tells a corny joke most.
Laughter rings through evening's veil,
With every chuckle, their colors pale.

Tulips gossip, sharing the scoop,
While daisies dance in a cheerful loop.
A funny world where blooms can play,
In a whimsical, wild ballet!

Delicate Secrets in Bloom

In gardens where giggles grow,
The daisies dance and put on a show.
With petals that tickle the sun,
They blush and shimmer, oh what fun!

Each bloom has a secret to share,
A funny tale of winds and fair.
Like butterflies with their sly little jokes,
They whisper softly, oh how it pokes!

The tulips tease with colors bright,
They laugh at bees, those busy sprites.
Three little buds with a wink and a sway,
Say, "We're the stars of the floral ballet!"

In this garden, laughter does rhyme,
With honeyed scents and a splash of thyme.
So join in the fun, don't be a pest,
For nature's giggles are truly the best!

When Flowers Whisper Love

A rose thought it was quite the charmer,
But lilies laughed, "Oh, what a farmer!"
Their petals fluffed in the breezy air,
Making secrets, without a care.

Tulips giggled beneath the sun,
"Why has the bee come for a pun?"
With nectar sweet and jokes galore,
They beckon love with a floral score!

The violets chimed in with glee,
"Did you hear what the daffodils agreed?"
They bowed their heads, a shy little gawk,
"We've got the best opening night talk!"

Amidst the petals, the laughter swells,
Nature's choir in the fragrant spells.
Whispers of love with a humorous twist,
A tapestry of colors wrapped in jest!

Traces of Spring's Tender Touch

Spring tiptoed in with a soft little grin,
Leaving trails of laughter as it began.
Through meadows and fields, it played all day,
Leaving flowers to giggle and sway.

The orchids conspired, plotting with glee,
"Who can wear the best smile? Let's see!"
With every bloom in a colorful spree,
It's a contest no flower would dare to flee!

In the evening, the petals would sigh,
Trading stories beneath the sky.
"Why do tulips always stand tall?"
"Because they don't want to trip and fall!"

And as the sun dipped down low,
The blossoms spun tales in the afterglow.
With jokes blooming bright, they danced in delight,
Spring's tender embrace made everything right!

Soft Petals and Sweet Dreams

In the moonlight, petals softly beam,
Whispering secrets of a sweet dream.
The nightingale sings, with humor so wide,
While daisies giggle at the garden's pride.

"Why did the flower refuse to chat?"
"Because it was giddy under a hat!"
With every buzz and fluttering wing,
Laughter echoed like it's the best spring fling.

The marigolds sported their golden crowns,
As roses wore laughter instead of frowns.
Under twinkling stars, their jokes took flight,
In a world where petals giggle all night!

With dreams woven from scents divine,
The garden's humor began to entwine.
So, if you stroll through the moonlit scene,
Watch for the petals that giggle and preen!

Dawn's Gentle Flush

The sun peeks in, a cheeky sprite,
Waking flowers with morning light.
They yawn and stretch, their petals wide,
As bees buzz in with chubby pride.

A daisy slips, its stem a twist,
It lands with grace, or so it wished.
A tulip giggles, tipsy sway,
As morning's laughter joins the play.

With every bloom, a joke unfurls,
As nature's jest is shared with whirls.
The breeze tickles, the branches laugh,
While dandelions act up, on behalf!

Then suddenly, a petal slips,
The flowers burst in fits and quips.
In this bouquet of merry cheer,
Dawn's gentle blush, what fun is here!

Threads of Radiance in Evening

In twilight's glow, the colors clash,
A flower wears its very best sash.
The roses strut with flair and pride,
While violets giggle, trying to hide.

A sunflower tilts, thinks it's a star,
While lilacs whisper, 'How bizarre!'
The jasmine swoons, a fragrant tease,
Rolling on petals like it's a breeze.

Amidst the hues, the laughter grows,
As evening's canvas playfully glows.
Nature's palette, with smirks in the air,
Threads of delight, beyond compare.

The winds play tricks with every bloom,
While petals fall, they dance in gloom.
In evening's theater, chaos spins,
As every flower wears silly grins.

The Language of Blossoms

In gardens grand, the whispers play,
Each bloom a tale in bright array.
The buttercups chat, so full of cheer,
While daisies gossip, their friendship clear.

A poppy winks, a daring tease,
While orchids flaunt, 'Oh, we're a breeze!'
The petals flutter, secrets shared,
In this floral world, all are prepared.

The violets script a comedy,
While azaleas plot an oddity.
Through blooms and scents, the jokes take flight,
In nature's script, nothing's contrite.

The language blooms, in colors bright,
As flowers chuckle in sheer delight.
In this blooming jest of sure finesse,
Each petal's punchline is pure happiness.

Soft Shades of Love's Arrival

When spring appears, love's playful tease,
With petals soft and dancing breeze.
The lilies prance, two-step in time,
As lavender hums a silly rhyme.

The tulip blushes, a rosy glance,
While honeysuckle sways in a trance.
A crocus slips, stumbles in glee,
As springtime teases with goofy spree.

With pastels bright, the flowers sing,
Tales of love, and joy they bring.
The daffodils cheer, with laughter loud,
In this soft shade, feel how it's proud!

Amidst the blooms, all hearts collide,
Soft shades of love, so sprightly, wide.
An annual jest, this beautiful dance,
As nature chuckles, in sweet romance.

The Color of Innocence

In the garden, petals sway,
A butterfly steals the show today.
With a giggle, it flutters near,
Whispering secrets we all can hear.

A tulip tries to make a joke,
But gets stuck on the word 'poke.'
The daisies laugh, they find it neat,
As petals crumple from the heat.

Roses blush, but we all know,
It's just from the sun's bright glow.
The violets snicker, sharing glee,
"Who knew flowers could be so free?"

So let's dance with laughter here,
Amidst the blooms, let's shed a tear.
For every petal that falls and slips,
There's joy in nature, hugs, and quips.

Serenade of the Blooming Hearth

In the garden, the sun turns up,
Where daisies drip from a teacup.
Lilies sing to the buzzing bee,
"Don't drink too much – you'll lose your key!"

A sunflower raises its leafy arm,
Calling out for a floral charm.
But the roses, with their pompous flair,
Just shake their heads and toss their hair.

Fluffy clouds drift above the trees,
"Hey, watch it!" says a leaf in the breeze.
The tulips try to form a band,
But no one can find the drumstick hand.

So let's laugh under the bright blue sky,
While flower friends pass on by.
Each petal a tale, each stem a cheer,
A serenade that all can hear!

Garden of Enchanted Awakenings

In a garden where giggles bloom,
A gnome awakens from his gloom.
"Hey, where's my hat?" he shouts with glee,
A wildflower responds, "Look under me!"

The daisies wear their hats too tight,
Complaining jesters in morning light.
"Who knew we'd start a fashion trend?
Now all the weeds just want to blend!"

Sunflowers strut like a fancy crowd,
Waving at bees, feeling quite proud.
"The nectar here is top-tier gold!"
"We're blossoming legends, so behold!"

With laughter echoing in sweet array,
Colorful blooms brighten the day.
In this garden, joy is spry,
Where every petal can reach the sky.

Caress of the Floral Whisper

Beneath the sun, the petals play,
Whispers dart on a breeze's way.
"Is that a weed, or just my friend?"
"Oh, just my luck, my roots won't bend!"

A bumblebee with a wiggly dance,
Takes a chance on a wobbly prance.
"Careful, friend, you might trip and fall!
Not all the flowers are having a ball!"

Dandelions puff in cheerful jest,
"Who needs rules? We're all the best!"
With every laugh, the garden shakes,
While nature plays its little pranks.

So let's twirl in this floral spree,
Where giggles blend like honeyed tea.
Each whisper shared, a charming tune,
In our garden of laughter, we bloom!

Veil of Pink Petals

In the garden, petals dance,
Drawing giggles at first glance.
Bees wear hats, oh what a sight,
Chasing blooms with sheer delight.

Napping blooms in the warm sun,
Whisper jokes, it's all in fun.
Petal parties on the ground,
With silly secrets all around.

Leaves wear shades of vivid hues,
While bunnies put on their best shoes.
They hop around with silly glee,
In this floral jubilee.

So if you see a flower grin,
Join the laughter, let's all spin.
For in this garden, joy takes root,
And chuckles grow with every shoot.

Heartbeats Among the Flowers

Swaying petals, comical show,
Heartbeats drumming, yes, just so.
Laughter stirs the sleepy breeze,
As daisies tease the bumblebees.

Oh, look at that dandelion's thought,
Wishing on dreams that can't be bought.
Each tiny seed wishes to run,
Off to chase some wacky fun.

Tulips wear their polka dots,
Tickling toes, they have the shots.
A funny little worm takes a twirl,
Making bees giggle, give a whirl.

Underneath the laughing trees,
Joyful blooms dance as they please.
In this garden, where humor grows,
Each heartbeat sings, and laughter flows.

When Buds Speak in Color

When buds chat, it's a riotous scene,
Colors shout, "Look at me, I'm green!"
Roses jokingly roll their eyes,
At sunflowers strutting with tall ties.

Petals gossip about the rain,
Silly stories, never mundane.
A bee buzzes in with a grin,
"Did you hear the one about the spin?"

Marigolds chuckle, so delightful,
Tickled by squirrels, oh so frightful.
As they squabble for the best sun,
In this blooming race, we all have fun.

So next time you see flowers tease,
Know they're sharing laughter with ease.
In this vibrant, colorful show,
Joy is the secret that they sow.

Radiant Secrets of the Garden

In the garden, whispers sweet,
Petals share their tales, upbeat.
A daffodil calls out with glee,
"Who needs sunlight? I'm so free!"

Hummingbirds boast, they fly so fast,
While daisies giggle at the past.
"Remember when we tripped on dew?"
"Oh yes," the lilies chuckle too!

Petal puns float on the air,
With butterfly jokes everywhere.
"Tulip's got a great punchline,"
Said a rose, nearly lost in thyme.

When blossoms gather, fun's in sight,
Their playful banter brings delight.
Radiant secrets they confide,
In this garden, laughter won't hide.

The Debut of Midnight Petals

In the garden, blossoms sway,
Dancing like they lost their way.
A petal fell, it made a sound,
"Oops! I tripped!"—the flowers browned.

Bees are buzzing, quite the show,
Chasing blooms, oh where'd they go?
A hummingbird with quite a flair,
Trips on nectar, flies through air!

With the dew comes silly cheer,
Daisies giggle, wiping tears.
A tulip told a joke so sly,
That even roses couldn't cry!

So let's raise a joyful cheer,
To blossoms bright, so full of cheer!
They might trip, they might fall flat,
But give them joy, and look at that!

Secrets in Nature's Colors

In the woods, colors collide,
A patchwork quilt, they can't hide.
Yellow daisies tell a tale,
Of how bluebells lose their trail.

The violets burst with giggles bright,
"Watch us twirl in morning light!"
Lilies wink with powdered grace,
While poppies join the crazy race.

What do trees and flowers know?
Secrets whispered in the grow.
"Let's paint the world, all hues we've got!"
Together they're a vibrant lot!

So here's a toast to nature's art,
With colors bold, they steal the heart.
In the fields, they dance with glee,
Those laughing petals wild and free!

Charms of the Springtime Heart

Springtime skips, a playful sprite,
With petals dancing, pure delight.
A dandelion makes a wish,
"I hope to taste a flower dish!"

Butterflies in silly flight,
Chasing colors, what a sight!
"Caught you!" giggled the daffodil,
"But I'll just play; I'm never still!"

The tulips stand, a fuzzy guard,
"Oh dear bees, please work real hard!"
But bees just laugh and roll around,
Swapping tales without a sound.

A chorus of blooms fills the air,
With silly tunes that barely care.
Nature's charms, they never part,
Springtime laughter fills the heart!

Hues of Spring's First Glance

Peeking out from winter's gloom,
Colors burst, like living bloom.
A shy crocus, just a poke,
Says, "Where's the party?"—oh, what a joke!

With every bud, a giggle grows,
As blushing petals steal the show.
A ladybug on its grand spree,
Shimmies past each flowering bee.

Jokes are whispered 'neath the trees,
While squirrels dance with perfect ease.
And in their hearts—a secret spark,
A chuckle shared across the park.

So with every petal's glance,
Springtime winks as flowers dance.
A funny tale in all those hues,
Nature's laugh, we can't refuse!

Dancing Shadows on Flowered Paths

In gardens where the daisies sway,
The shadows chuckle, dance and play.
Giggling petals, in the breeze,
Whisper secrets to the trees.

The bees are buzzing, quite the show,
They wobble left and dip to low.
Chasing butterflies with style,
In this floral, funny mile.

With every stomp, the dirt flies high,
A little mud, a goofy sigh.
But laughter's planted all around,
In this quirky, blooming ground.

So skip along the flowered trail,
Find joy in petals, bright and pale.
For life's too short, let's laugh and hop,
With dancing shadows, never stop!

The Love Language of Gardens

Roses talk in fragrant tones,
While daisies giggle, in funny zones.
A tulip twirls with every glance,
In this sweet, blooming romance.

Lavender whispers soft and low,
In playful jests, it steals the show.
Sunflowers wink with golden glee,
Spreading cheer, just wait and see.

Petunias plot a cheeky scheme,
To brighten up the gardener's dream.
Snapdragons tease with a silly grin,
In this garden, love's a whim!

So next time you take a stroll,
Listen close; plants have a role.
For love's not just between the leaves,
It's laughter, joy, and what it weaves!

Heartstrings Tied to Floral Dreams

In dreams where flowers dance in rows,
The violets giggle, and the lily glows.
Every petal whispers, 'Hey, look here!'
While silly thoughts are often near.

A dandelion's wish flies away,
To tickle clouds in a goofy play.
It dreams of being a grand bouquet,
With laughs that drift and sway all day.

The marigolds wear silly hats,
While mockingbirds sing fun chats.
In this world of blooms that tease,
Life's a joke, with flowers at ease.

So tie your heart with a stem of cheer,
In floral dreams, the laughter's dear.
With every bloom, just dance and sway,
For joy's the bloom that lights the way!

The Colors of a Quiet Sun

When the sun shines in quiet hues,
It tickles flowers, bright and bruised.
Pinks and yellows start to roam,
In the garden, they feel at home.

Petals giggle under golden rays,
As squirrels scamper in their plays.
A pansy, wearing a purple frown,
Finds laughter, turning upside down.

The sun, a painter with a brush,
Creates such warmth in a gentle rush.
But watch it spill, a jazzy spree,
Splashing colors, wild and free.

So when the quiet sun sets low,
Let's dance among the blooms that glow.
With silly shades and hearty cheer,
In floral sunsets, joy is near!

The Lipstick of Nature

In the garden, colors play,
Nature's palette on display.
A pink petal winks, oh so sly,
A flirt with the breeze, passing by.

With a cheeky grin, flowers sing,
Each shade a whisper, a secret fling.
A flower's kiss, a bee's delight,
They laugh together, what a sight!

Daisies in polka dots, feeling fine,
Tulips sipping nectar like wine.
Nature's lipstick, bold and bright,
Painting joy from morning to night.

In this play, no need for rules,
Just petals and laughter amongst the fools.
With every bloom, each giggling hue,
Nature's charm, forever anew.

Tints of Desire Under Sunlight

Sunlight dances, in colors galore,
A flicker, a shimmer, who could ask for more?
Roses in red, like a cheeky tease,
Petals giggle, swaying with ease.

Dandelions puff, with wild delight,
They tickle the sun, in laughter's flight.
Cacti in green, with an attitude bold,
Winking at wanderers, stories untold.

Violets whisper secrets at noon,
Caught in a game of hide-and-seek tunes.
A sunflower's grin, so bright and wide,
Waving at bees, with a boisterous pride.

Under the warmth, every hue shines,
Creating a canvas where humor intertwines.
Nature's palette, a painter's dream,
Crafting a laughter-filled sunbeam.

Blushing Gardens at Dusk

As dusk flirts with the fading light,
Gardens chuckle, what a sight!
Lavender blushes in the flame's glow,
While daisies giggle, putting on a show.

Crickets join in, strumming their strings,
While evening wraps up its pastel flings.
The moon peeks through, like a shy friend,
Nature's laughter, a blend without end.

Lilies leap into twilight's embrace,
With a wink and a twirl, they join the race.
Whispers of petals, tales in the air,
Their stories drift without a care.

In this hour, where shadows blend,
The gardens blush, and laughter transcends.
A symphony of petals, soft and sweet,
As day's laughter finds its retreat.

Petal Poetry in the Breeze

In the whispering wind, petals dance,
Flaunting their shades, taking a chance.
A daisy's head tosses, a bashful grin,
Flirting with clouds, let the fun begin!

Chasing the laughter of butterflies too,
Every bloom giddy, as if it knew.
Petals pirouette, a captivating sight,
Glorious mischief, in broad daylight.

Hydrangeas boast in light blue attire,
With hues so bold, they never tire.
A flirt with the breeze, they sway and tease,
Oh, what a world, where petals appease.

Nature's poems write laughter untold,
In every fold and bloom, bright and bold.
In this garden of giggles, hearts skip a beat,
As petals compose their rhythm, oh so sweet.

Nature's Gentle Tinctures

In gardens bright with laughter's hue,
The daisies giggled, how about you?
The bees wore stripes like a fashion show,
While ladybugs danced to the breezy flow.

The tulips pranced in their vibrant skirts,
Claiming victory over the dirt.
With pollen tickles, the flowers tease,
As butterflies waltz on the gentle breeze.

Echoes of Velvet Petals

Petals whisper secrets, pink and shy,
They chuckle softly as they wave goodbye.
The roses blush when a bee goes near,
And tulips blush too, but who has no fear?

A sunflower grins, its face in the sun,
Saying, 'Who knew being bright was so fun?'
Clover conspiracies grow down below,
With a wink and a nudge, they steal the show.

The Awakening of Color

The sky paints giggles with each morning light,
While flowers yawn wide, what a funny sight!
The violets chuckle, the lilacs tease,
A rainbow of humor sways with the breeze.

Every bloom has a story to share,
Of naughty ants plotting without a care.
With laughter and colors that dance in delight,
Spring brings a chuckle, a whimsical sight.

Whispered Wishes of Cherry Trees

Cherry trees giggle in rosy delight,
As petals rain down, oh what a sight!
With wishes afloat on a breeze of cheer,
They blush at the thought of their fruits being near.

Squirrels chatter, plotting a feast,
While birds chirp tunes for the colorful beast.
With pink confetti, the front yard's aglow,
Who knew nature's joke could steal the show?

Petal Dreams in Twilight's Glow

In the garden where giggles play,
Petals twirl like they're on holiday.
A bee with dance moves, quite absurd,
Sipping nectar, not a care in the world.

Colorful blooms with secrets to share,
Tickling each other, a mischievous air.
A butterfly trip, did you see that slip?
Landing with flair, was it all just a quip?

With each petal drifting, whispers arise,
"Oh no, it's me! I've lost my disguise!"
And the sun chuckles, what a fine view,
As flowers gossip, trying to construe.

In twilight's embrace, laughter takes flight,
Floral friendships painted in twilight.
It's a riot of colors, a humorous band,
Where petals unite, it's perfectly planned.

Tranquil Shades of First Light

When dawn breaks, the flowers declare,
"We've overslept! What a futile affair!"
With yawns and stretches, they rise from the bed,
Chasing away dreams of a snail on its head.

Sunbeams sneak in with a cheeky shout,
"Hello, sleepyheads! It's time to sprout!"
Yet petals, still dazed, might just refuse,
To open their eyes, they've nothing to lose.

A dew droplet giggles, "I could squeeze in!"
"Just don't wake the rose, she's lost in a spin!"
But daisies are ready, with jokes to impart,
As they whisper, "Fresh starts can be quite the art!"

Bright hues in the morning, blossoms all aglow,
Sharing tales of last night's hilarious show.
They dance in delight, a whimsical sight,
In tranquil first light, everything feels right.

The Serenade of Swaying Stems

In a breeze, the stems begin to sway,
"Is it a dance or a game we play?"
Silly leaf said, "Let's show our flair!"
With roots tapping out a catchy affair.

Swaying side to side, petals offbeat,
Making the ground ripple beneath their feet.
"Oh, watch this move!" cried a daring shoot,
Till a gust of wind left him quite mute.

"Watch me flip, now watch me glide!"
Giggling flowers joined the wild ride.
With every twist and twirl in delight,
Spring's catchy tune makes everything light.

A flower pot DJ spins in the back,
Adding music to every flower attack.
They chuckle and cheer, it's a floral affair,
And the garden erupts into a sway without care.

Hues of a Secret Lover

Under the moon, the petals conspire,
Whispering secrets with a mischievous fire.
"Did you hear what the lilac said?"
"It was a shocking tale of a honeybee's dread!"

A daisy chuckled, "I saw it unfold,
With lavender blushes and stories retold!"
While violets giggled in a playful tease,
As colors merged under the night's gentle breeze.

"Oh, what a romance in the night's velvet cloak,
Where even the shadows are playing a joke!"
A wisteria sighed, "Oh love is mad sweet!
What if our blooms made a charming retreat?"

In hues of desire, the jokes intertwine,
As petals play tricks, oh how they do shine!
The garden, a canvas, in laughter immersed,
With hues of affection, their joys are conversed.

The Gentle Caress of Flora

In a garden where the daisies grin,
A bee told a flower, "Let the games begin!"
They giggled like kids, in a playful spree,
Dancing on petals, wild and free.

The tulips looked on, with a wry little smile,
"You think you're so sweet, but we're more versatile!"
The roses chimed in, with colors so bright,
"We're the flowers that always steal the spotlight!"

A dandelion chuckled, all puffy and round,
"I'll blow you kisses and scatter around!"
The violets just sighed, in lavender glee,
"We're all in this laugh-fest, just wait and see!"

As evening approached, the petals took flight,
We waved them goodnight, under stars shining bright.
Tomorrow they'd gather, for another round,
In the garden where giggles are always found.

Swaying in Tenderness

In the breeze, a daffodil swayed,
Telling the tulips, "I just made a trade!"
"Some of my sunshine, for a touch of your hue,"
The tulips just laughed, "That deal is on you!"

A lilac overheard and chimed in with cheer,
"I'll dance along, come twirl with me here!"
The hydrangeas nodded, in pastel delight,
With petals like candy, they twinkled at night.

They swayed to the rhythm of nature's sweet tune,
While a squirrel spun around, under the moon.
With berries as treats, they all shared a bite,
Nature was giggling, all through the night!

When morning arrived, they stretched and they grinned,
"More antics await! Are you all ready, friends?"
And so with good humor, they welcomed the day,
In their playful embrace, come what may!

The First Kiss of the Sun

Oh, the sun peeked in with a glorious flair,
Whispering secrets to blossoms that dare.
"Time to rise up, with a sparkle and shine!"
The petals all blushed, saying, "Oh, you're divine!"

A sunflower grinned, standing oh-so-tall,
"Kiss me good morning, I'll gladly enthrall!"
Daisy called back, "Don't hog all the light!"
And the sun just chuckled, "I'm here, hold on tight!"

The rays tickled leaves, making them dance,
While the jumping grasshoppers took a wild chance.
A ladybug giggled, her stripes all aglow,
"I'll join in the fun, where the laughter can flow!"

As noon held its reign, in a warm, golden hue,
They shared silly stories, as good friends do.
And though the day wandered, they stayed close at heart,
For each sunlit moment was a fabulous part.

Nature's Blushing Heartbeat

The streams chuckled softly, with bubbles that play,
Telling the flowers, "We're here to stay!"
Every ripple echoed with laughter and cheer,
"Join in our chorus, come close and draw near!"

The trees wagged their branches, with mischief in thought,
"We'll tickle the clouds, just give it a shot!"
The wind piped in, with a wink in its blow,
"I'll shake up your petals and steal the show!"

A butterfly danced, on a wobbly path,
"Catch me if you can! Come join in my laugh!"
The daisies all giggled, their faces in bloom,
"We'll race to the finish, let's banish all gloom!"

As twilight approached, there was joy all around,
Nature's heartbeat echoed, melodic and sound.
In a world full of wonder, where humor prevails,
Every moment together, a story that sails.

The Silken Touch of Life

In the garden where giggles bloom,
Butterflies flutter, dancing in room.
A bee in a tux, oh what a sight,
Buzzing in style, a real delight!

Petals prance in a playful race,
Winking at clouds with a silly face.
Sunshine spills like fizzy soda,
Nature's party, oh what a moda!

With daisies wearing hats, oh so grand,
And tulips doing the conga, unplanned.
Grass tickles toes, laughter takes flight,
Life in this garden feels just right!

So let's raise a toast to this wild show,
Where flowers and fun constantly grow.
For every petal holds a giggle clear,
In this silly realm, let's bring good cheer!

Emotions of the Flowering Veil

Oh, the whispers of petals, so light,
Giggling at squirrels in sheer delight.
A daisy chimes, 'Oh, play me a tune!'
While roses blushing, try to swoon.

Fragrance swirls like a cheeky dance,
Snapdragons joke, give life a chance.
Lilies laugh, 'We're out of vogue!',
As violets tumble in a rogue fog.

The tulips gossip, oh what a fuss!
'Did you see how the bees made a fuss?'
With colors that clash, they prance and sway,
In this field of humor, they whisper all day.

So let the blooms take you on a ride,
Through giggles and hues, on joy's bright tide.
A bloom's wild heart will always avail,
In this garden of laughter, none can curtail!

In the Shade of Cherry Blossoms

Under pink clouds, what a sight,
Squirrels chitter with all their might.
A raccoon peeks, with a curious eye,
Seeing petals drip like a pie in the sky.

Breezes are teasing, they tickle and play,
Dancing through branches, they twirl and sway.
Cherry trees giggle, dropping their loot,
As folks below slip in floral pursuit!

A picnic blooms, with crumbs galore,
Beneath the pink canopy, laughter will soar.
"Oh dear!" someone squeals, as a blossom lands,
On their ice cream—what a sticky hand!

Here in this shade, where chuckles collide,
Life's sweetest moments bloom far and wide.
In the company of petals that thrill,
We gather our joy, oh what a thrill!

A Symphony of Petal Perfume

In petals' embrace, melodies sing,
Nature's own band, what joy they bring.
A breeze with notes, soft and sweet,
Invites all to dance, oh what a treat!

Sunshine giggles, tickling the leaves,
While flowers conspire in whimsy achieves.
Dandelions prank—'We're not weeds!'
Chasing the wind as the laughter proceeds.

With colors that clash in fanciful glee,
Each bloom is a jester; oh can't you see?
Petal perfumes swirl in a fragrant tune,
Carrying wishes, like kites to the moon.

As blossoms applaud in harmony bright,
The world revels in this joyful light.
A symphony flourishing, growing abound,
In laughter we find, life's magic is found!

The Rosy Embrace of Spring

In the park, a bee flies near,
A flower giggles, oh so clear.
"What a bumbling fool!" it calls,
The buzzing buzz cuts through the thralls.

Petals sway, a dance so spry,
As laughter blooms beneath the sky.
The sun spills lemonade on the grass,
While squirrels plot, their antics a class.

A bouquet tries to stand so tall,
But its stems begin to fall.
"I need support, or just a friend!"
The daisies whisper, "Well, we can pretend!"

With colors splashed in cheerful hues,
The flowers gossip, sharing news.
"Who wore petals best?" they tease,
As bees just shrug, buzzing with ease.

Secrets Beneath Cherry Leaves

Underneath where shadows play,
A giggling leaf whispers the day.
"Did you hear the tulips' joke?"
"I'm all ears!" a seedling spoke.

A wily bud leans in to say,
"Why did the rose go on a spree?
To avoid being pruned in such a way,
And dance with bees, oh so carefree!"

The petals chuckle, the sunlight beams,
While dandelions plot wacky schemes.
"Let's race the wind, who'll be the first?"
A comical pluck, and off they burst!

As whispers swirl while skies turn teal,
The flowers trade jokes with dainty zeal.
"Let's write a poem! It'll be a hoot!"
Their laughter rises, a hallowed fruit.

Cerise Skylines at Dawn

As dawn tiptoes on rose-tipped toes,
The clouds blush pink, creating shows.
"Look! A cotton candy sky!"
The sun chuckles, a cheeky guy.

Cardinals sing a melody sweet,
While daffodils tap dance on their feet.
"What's the best joke you know?" one asked,
"Why did the petunia wear a mask?"

"Because it was afraid of being a wallflower,
And didn't want some bee to cower!"
The blossoms roar with laughter loud,
As petals twirl, all brightly proud.

Sky-high giggles fill the morn,
As dew drops laugh at the seeds forlorn.
With morning's glow, the fun has begun,
In floral antics, we bask in sun.

Dance of the Floral Veils

A lilac spins, so fine, so bright,
With polka dots, it's quite the sight.
"Watch me twirl in morning air!"
Said a petal with a flair.

"Did you hear, the cosmos tried to dance?"
It stepped on toes in floral France.
"Oh dear, what a fumble, what a fall!"
The daisies giggle, echoing the call.

A tulip trips but waves inspired,
"Catch me, bloom! My dreams are wired!"
As butterflies applaud the show,
The garden bursts with laughter's glow.

Through the dance, the blooms all sigh,
With twinkling winks they flutter by.
"Who needs perfection? Let's be fun!"
As petals cheer the rising sun.

The Scent of Hope Unfurled

In a garden where giggles bloom,
A flower sneezed, and oh what gloom.
Bees in hats danced all around,
While tulips swayed to a silly sound.

Petals painted with shades of cheer,
Each one whispers, 'Spring is here!'
A daffodil tried a cartwheel too,
But tripped on its stem, oh what a view!

Every bud tries to tell a joke,
Even the daisies, they gently poke.
"Why did the rose cross the lane?
To get to the garden's next champagne!"

As laughter sprouts from each new leaf,
Nature's comedy, a sweet relief.
In this patch of whimsical glee,
Hope unfurls, come join the spree!

Delicate Radiance of Spring's Kiss.

The squirrels wear tiny hats in style,
While daffodils cheer and smile.
A snail on a skateboard zooms by fast,
"Watch out," yells a tulip, "Get off, you rascal!"

Sunshine drips like honey gold,
Each petal's secret just begs to be told.
A lily wiggles, a peony prances,
Together they start a dance of glances.

Grasshoppers doth wear bow ties neat,
While butterflies settle with dainty feet.
"Is it spring?" asks the sweet bumblebee,
"Or are we all just quirky?" Ah, so free!

With laughter we twirl in the light,
Nature's joy feels just so right.
Here in the sun's warm embrace,
Every little giggle finds its place.

Petals in Scarlet

A gardener stood with a watering can,
Looking for weeds, with a sneaky plan.
"Oh look, a puffy cloud!" he did claim,
But it's just a cauliflower playing the game!

Petals blush in a comical show,
Like shy kids caught in the first row.
"Why are we red?" asks a rose with flair,
"Because we've eaten too much rhubarb, I swear!"

A marigold giggles, "I dare you to dare,
To dance in the breeze, not a worry nor care!"
The daisies gather, planning a prank,
"Let's tickle the tulips, let's draw in a plank!"

Frogs in tuxedos croak out a tune,
As shadows play till the rise of the moon.
Here in this floral, funny delight,
Each petal's a star, shining through the night.

Whispering Petal Dreams

A thistle dreams of being a queen,
While violets giggle at the scene.
"Who said a thorn can't wear a crown?"
Every flower chuckles, "Let's all sit down!"

On a breeze, the pollen flies high,
As the daisies plot to reach the sky.
A bumblebee buzzes a funny song,
"Guys, let's party, we've waited too long!"

Pansies wear shades, acting so cool,
While sunflowers dance in the schoolyard rule.
"Which one's the best?" asks a sweet petunia,
"Let's all be ourselves, that's the true funia!"

Sprinkling laughter across the green,
Nature's charm, the funniest scene.
In a world where smiles are the theme,
Whispering dreams, like petals, redeem!

The Floral Masquerade of Spring

In the garden, flowers prance,
Wearing colors, a bright dance.
Daisies giggle, tulips sway,
As bees waltz, without delay.

The sun peeks, a playful tease,
Twirling petals in the breeze.
Lilies wear their fanciest hats,
While the pansies chuckle at spats.

A rose sneezes, blooms take flight,
Caught in pollen's sneaky plight.
Tulips trade their fragrant jokes,
While sunflowers play hide-and-poke.

Oh, the fun that nature brings,
In this floral mask, everyone sings.
With laughter bright as spring's warm glow,
Dancing petals steal the show!

The Sweet Sigh of Blossoms

In the park, sweet scents arrive,
As blossoms giggle and thrive.
Petals whisper, 'What a day!'
While bees buzz secrets, come what may.

Cherry trees in a pink parade,
Sporting blooms like a fancy braid.
'Look at us!' the violets shout,
Their little voices full of clout.

The sun sneezes, spreading rays,
While daisies dance in sunlit bays.
Each color tries to outshine the rest,
With nature's art, oh how they're blessed!

So here we bask in nature's cheer,
As flowers prattle all year.
A laughter shared through petals light,
In their sweet sighs, the joy ignites!

Nature's Gentle Caress

Little buds peek from the ground,
With soft giggles, joy abounds.
A gentle breeze puffs out its cheeks,
As flowers share their playful tweaks.

Wisteria swings from overhead,
Tickling noses that dare to tread.
Hummingbirds zip around for tea,
While the daisies chuckle with glee.

Buttercups gather in a huddle,
Comparing hues and floral muddle.
The violets pout, 'Where's our fame?'
But forget their frowns with game after game.

Nature's laughter rings out clear,
As blossoms spread the cheer.
In this playful, fragrant bliss,
Each petal whispers a comical kiss!

Tender Tints and Floral Whispers

In the meadow, colors collide,
Flowers giggling, side by side.
Fuchsia jokes with the sunflower,
While daisies grin, singing with power.

Petals blush with laughter bright,
As bumblebees take comedic flight.
Each hue whispers tales anew,
While playful breezes swoop and flew.

Roses chuckle, 'We're the champs!'
While violets roll like little tramps.
Tulips strut in their springy shoes,
Dancing to nature's quirky blues.

Oh, the fun these blooms can share,
In this whimsical flowery affair.
With every hue and playful grin,
Spring revels where smiles begin!

Laughter in Bloom

In springtime's glow, the flowers jest,
They tickle the bees with their bright little zest.
A daisy said, 'Hey! I've got a joke!'
The tulips giggled, and then they spoke!

With petals like skirts, they whirl around,
Spreading their laughter, a joy profound.
The sunbeams chuckle, the raindrops prance,
While daisies wiggle in a frolicsome dance.

Clover joins in with a shy little grin,
As violets tease, "Aren't we all kin?"
Jokes in the garden, a riotous spree,
Nature's own laugh track, wild and free!

Petals are pillows, so soft and so sweet,
In this flower patch, life's a comical treat.
Giggles abound, as the squirrels all play,
In laughter's embrace, we frolic away.

The Dance of Flora's Heart

In the meadow's arena, the flowers collide,
A sunflower twirls with an elegant stride.
The roses are gossiping, oh such a scene,
While pansies join in with a flip and routine!

Each daisy declares, "Look at my flair!"
The buttercups blush with their golden glare.
"Who's got the moves?" they all start to boast,
While bumblebees buzz like a party host.

Carnations chuckle with rhythm and rhyme,
With petals all dancing, they're having a time.
"Spin, little buds! Show us your best!"
Nature's our DJ, bringing the zest!

As twilight descends, the petals still sway,
Under the starlight, they dance and they play.
In the symphony of spring, laughter's the art,
A whimsical jamboree, the dance of the heart.

A Canvas of Springtime Echoes

On the canvas of spring, with colors so bright,
A funny refrain takes its flight in the light.
"Hey flower!" calls out a cheeky young bud,
"Let's paint the air, with laughter and mud!"

With brush strokes of petals, they color the skies,
Each hue brings a chuckle, as one flower tries.
"Oops! I dripped blue!" cries a crocus in woe,
While lilies just giggle, "Well, go with the flow!"

The daisies doodle with lines all askew,
Creating a masterpiece, silly yet true.
"Art is subjective!" they cleverly cheer,
As worms join the fun, with a squirm and a sneer.

The wind carries whispers of laughter and jest,
In this colorful patch, life's truly the best.
A canvas of spring where the echoes unite,
Painting joy in the garden, both day and night.

Secrets Beneath the Petal's Skin

Beneath the soft petals, secrets reside,
A tulip confides, "I once took a ride!"
The daisies all gasp, "Oh, do tell us more!"
"On a bumblebee's back, I soared and I swore!"

The roses gossip, with whispers so sly,
"Did you hear about daisies who dream to fly?"
"Sorry!" chirps one, "We'd rather just sway,
In this garden of giggles, we dance every day!"

The lilacs exchange all their humorous tales,
Of funny little bugs, and their wiggly wails.
"Last week, I tripped over my own two leaves!"
"In this flowery world, even flowers have grieves!"

So secrets are shared in the bloom of the bright,
As petals reveal laughter, bringing pure delight.
With each little secret tucked under the sun,
In the garden of whimsy, we're all here for fun!

www.ingramcontent.com/pod-product-compliance
Lightning Source LLC
Chambersburg PA
CBHW072143200426
43209CB00051B/357